No RAiN,

No FLOWERS

THOMAS LÉLU

NO RAIN,

NO FLOWERS

THOMAS LÉLU

An Introduction to Thomas Lélu

WHAT DOES 'NO RAIN, NO FLOWERS' SYMBOLISE FOR YOU?

'No Rain, No Flowers' – means the good weather that comes after the rain and vice versa, but it can also remind you to stay optimistic whatever happens…

WHY DID YOU START WRITING BIRO NOTES?

I started writing notes biro every day, to pass them on and share my vision of life.

WHAT DO YOU LIKE ABOUT BIROS?

I like writing in biro because it is gentle, imperfect, fragile and universal.

WHAT DO YOU LIKE MOST ABOUT BOOKS?

My favorite thing about books is the smell of the paper.

HOW CAN WE ALL BE MORE CREATIVE?

We can all be creative if we never stop being curious and work every day. It's both discipline and fun.

HOW HAS THE SOCIAL MEDIA LANDSCAPE CHANGED THE WAY WE CONSUME ART?

Social networks allow artists to show their work to a wider audience, with the risk that this work is diluted in the mass, it is an opportunity and a trap at the same time.

Follow me @ThomasLelu for more digital musings.

WHAT GETS YOU UP IN THE MORNING?

Birdsong.

WHAT IS THE ONE LINER YOU LIVE FOR LIFE?

- Morning!

- no, thanks.

WHAT IS THE MEANING OF LIFE?

Life is love.

EVERYTHING
PASSES.

EVERYTHINGS
CHANGES.
JUST DO
WHAT YOU
THINK
YOU SHOULD
DO!

MORE THAN

FRIENDS

LESS THAN

~~FRIEND~~ LOVERS

— DO YOU THINK
MEN ARE
    IMPORTANT?

— LIKE, FOR WHAT?

GOOD THINGS
HAPPEN WHEN
YOU SMILE
OR WHEN
YOU'RE
NAKED.

PLEASE DON'T INTERRUPT ME WHILE I'M IGNORING YOU.

GET MONEY FIRST
FALL IN LOVE
LATER.

ASK YOURSELF THIS:
WHO THE
FUCK
CARES ?

FEELING SAD
AND DEPRESSED?

YOU MIGHT
BE SUFFERING
FROM
CAPITALISM.

NOBODY
CARES
ABOUT
YOUR FAKE
LIFE ON
SOCIAL
MEDIA.

SORRY BUT I DON'T
ANSWER PRIVATE
NUMBERS.

OR NUMBERS THAT
I DON'T KNOW

OR ANYONE EVER.

Also, DON'T
CALL ME.

LOVE YOUR

FUCKING LIFE

MAY BE
MEMORY

is ALL THE
HOME
YOU GET.

A POEM FOR MONDAYS

COFFEE

COFFEE

COFFEE, COFFEE

EVERYONE SHUT UP!

COFFEE

EVERYTHING
PASSES.

EVERYTHINGS
CHANGES.
JUST DO
WHAT YOU
THINK
YOU SHOULD
DO!

I TOLERATE

YOU .

DO MORE
THINGS
THAT MAKE
YOU FORGET
TO CHECK
YOUR PHONE!

— SOMETIMES
I LIKE
TO GO TO
THE GYM TO
LOOK AT
MY PHONE.

I LIKE YOU

BUT I HATE

YOUR

INSTAGRAM

STORIES

Hello !

I'M TRYING

MY   BEST .

Let's take pics

we can

never

post.

BEAUTIFUL.

DEFINITION :

A PERSON WHO IS
        READING THIS

FUCK CAN
BE USED IN
MANY WAYS AND
is PROBABLY THE
ONLY FUCKING WORD
THAT CAN BE
PUT EVERY
FUCKING WHERE!

PEOPLE
WITH
MULTIPLE
PERSONALITIES
SHOULD DONATE
ONE OF THEM
TO PEOPLE WHO
DON'T HAVE
ONE!

I GET NERVOUS
BUT
I TRY MY
BEST

DON'T RUSH
INTO A
RELATIONSHIP
BE FRIENDS
FIRST. MAYBE
THEY HAVE
HOTTER
FRIENDS.

THANK ME
LATER

HERE WE
FUCKING
GO AGAIN

I MEAN
GOOD MORNING

I HAD
NOTHING
TO DO THIS
WEEK·END SO
I DECIDED
TO FALL IN
LOVE.

— CAN YOU
HEAR ME?

— NO IT'S
TOO
DARK .

THINGS TO DO
TODAY :

1 — WAKE UP

2 — SURVIVE

3 — GO BACK
TO BED

ALL
EMPLOYEES
MUST STOP
CRYING
BEFORE
RETURNING TO
WORK !

HOW ABOUT A NICE

CUP OF

~~SHUT~~ SHUT THE

FUCK UP?

I TOLD

MY THERAPIST

ABOUT

YOU

YOU'RE NOT DEEP

YOU'RE NOT AN
INTELLECTUAL

YOU'RE NOT AN
ARTIST

YOU'RE NOT A
CRITIC

YOU'RE NOT A
POET

YOU JUST HAVE
INTERNET ACCESS

IGNORE

THIS →

↑

IGNORE

THOSE

↗

IGNORE

THAT

↙

41

I CAN'T AFFORD TO HATE PEOPLE, I HAVEN'T GOT THAT KIND OF TIME.

DO YOURSELF

A FAVOR

AND DELETE

SOME people

FROM YOUR LIFE.

IF ANYONE HAS

ANY EXPERIENCE

WITH ANYTHING

OR KNOWS

ANYTHING PLEASE

LET ME KNOW.

FUCK

☐ YOU

☐ ME

☐ EVERYONE

WHAT DO YOU
            NEED RIGHT
                NOW ?

    _   A HUG.

I HAVE

2 MILESTONES

AT WORK:

1 — LUNCH

2 — LEAVING

WE'RE FUCKING
ARTISTS
WE'RE SENSITIVE
AS SHIT!

TODAY WE
DON'T HAVE ANY
MOTIVATIONAL
QUOTES, IF YOU
WANT TO
GIVE UP,
GIVE UP.

— YOU'RE BEAUTIFUL

— YOU'RE DRUNK

NOTHING IS NEW

TODAY

— JUST BE
YOURSELF...

— WHO IS THAT?

It's me

and my

4 hours of

sleep

against the

world.

WHEN I'M GOOD,

I'M VERY GOOD,

BUT WHEN

I'M BAD,

I'M BETTER.

I KNEW WHO
I WAS THIS
MORNING BUT
I CHANGED A
FEW TIMES
SINCE THEN.

MY HEART SAYS YES

MY BRAIN SAYS WTF

YOU'RE

DOING

YOUR

FUCKING

BEST.

BE WHO

YOU

NEEDED

WHEN YOU

WERE YOUNGER

— DID YOU DREAM
OF ME?

— I DIDN'T
DREAM,
I WAS too
TIRED.

RISK

ATTRACTS

TALENT

NOT EVERYTHING

HAS TO MAKE

SENSE.

LET IT GO.

CHOOSE

PEACE.

JUST BECAUSE
IT'S TAKING
TIME
DOESN'T MEAN
IT'S NOT
HAPPENING.

SOMETIMES

HOME is

A

 PERSON

FUCK STRESS

HAVE

SEX!

MY

FAVORITE

pLACE

is iNSiDE

YOUR ~~HUG~~

HUG

IN A
MAD
WORLD
ONLY THE
MAD
ARE
SANE.

NOT
ANTISOCIAL
JUST
SOCIALLY
SELECTIVE.

CREATE
A LIFE
YOU CAN'T
WAIT TO
WAKE UP TO

TAKE A RISK,

LIFE IS

BORING

HONEY.

LOVE IS A
FEELING
NOT A
DECISION

THE WORLD HAS
BIGGER PROBLEMS
THAN BOYS
WHO KISS
BOYS AND
GIRLS WHO
KISS GIRLS.

WHY DO SEXY
    PEOPLE (ME)
HAVE TO
    SUFFER SO
        MUCH?

I LOVE THE
3 AM VERSION
of PEOPLE:

1- VULNERABLE

2 - HONEST

3 - REAL

DATING TIPS :

DON'T .

FUCK
ME
I'M
TIRED

DEAR INSTAGRAM
PLEASE STOP
SUGGESTING PEOPLE
I MAY KNOW.

I KNOW THEM BUT

I DON'T LIKE
THEM.

GO HOME

AND MAKE

LOVE !

(IT'S AN ORDER)

MOOD:

MOVE to
ANOTER CitY
AND START
A NEW liFE.

IF IT MAKES
YOU HAPPY,
IT'S NOT
A WASTE
OF TIME.

I'M   THE
HAPPIEST
DEPRESSED
PERSON you'll
EVER   MEET.

DISAPPOINTED

BUT

NOT SURPRISED.

Life's too
SHORT,
TEll ME
You'RE IN
LoVE WITH
ME Now.

MY FAVOURITE
SEASON IS THE
FALL OF PATRIARCHY

SOMETIMES YOU
DON'T GET
WHAT YOU WANT
BECAUSE YOU

DESERVE BETTER

IF THIS IS
REALITY
I'M NOT
INTERESTED

POPULARITY IS FOR STUPID PEOPLE

It's Now

OR

NEVER

BEING
HUMAN
FEELS
SO HEAVY

MOST OF THE STUFF PEOPLE WORRY ABOUT NEVER HAPPENS

TO BE
WITH YOU
THAT'S ALL
I WANT

DESCRIBE YOURSELF
IN THREE
WORDS :

I AM A
REBEL

I WISH

I HAD

MORE

MIDDLE

FINGERS.

SOMETIMES
YOU JUST
HAVE TO
REST .
THE WORLD
CAN
WAIT.

I'M NOT
MYSELF
TODAY.
MAYBE
I'M YOU

I'M OUT
OF MY MIND
AT THIS TIME
BUT GO
AHEAD
AND LEAVE
A
MESSAGE

I HAD A

FLASH BACK

OF SOMETHING

THAT NEVER

EXISTED.

STOP COPYING
ME YOU'RE
NOT EVEN
DOING IT
RIGHT.

HATING POPULAR
THINGS
DOESN'T MAKE
YOU AN

INTERSTING
PERSON.

THE opposite
TO A

FEMINIST is
AN

ASSHOLE.

CLOSED
UNTIL

EVERYTHING
CALMS

DOWN

BE HERE NOW

THINGS I WANT:

1) YOU

2)

ADULT FRIENDSHIPS
BE LIKE
"I MISS YOU",
LET'S HANG OUT
IN JUNE.

MONDAYS
AREN'T SO BAD
IT'S YOUR
JOB THAT
SUCKS.

IT'S OK

TO

DISCONNECT

FOR

A WHILE

EXPECT
NOTHING

APPRECIATE
EVERYTHING

MOOD:

I JUST WANNA
SIT IN FRONT
OF THE OCEAN &
LISTEN TO THE
WAVES.

THANK
YOU FOR
LIKING
MY STUPID
POST

MONDAY

MONDAY 2

MONDAY 3

MONDAY 4

FRIDAY

SATURDAY

PRE-MONDAY

MEETING YOU WAS A NICE ACCIDENT

YOU

will

NEVER

FIND

ANOTHER

ME

DEAD
INSIDE
BUT STILL
HORNY

USE
THINGS
NOT PEOPLE.
LOVE
PEOPLE
NOT THINGS!

STOP TRYING
TO BE LIKED
BY EVERYBODY

YOU DON'T
EVEN LIKE

EVERYBODY

THE

BEST PART

OF MY

DAY IS

TALKING TO

YOU

MY BODY

ISN'T
FLAWED,
YOUR
THINKING
IS.

THE LOVE
YOU
GAVE
WAS
NEVER

A WASTE.

I FEEL BAD

FOR THE people

WHO NEVER

GO CRAZY.

PRIVACY IS POWER

WHAT PEOPLE DON'T KNOW, THEY CAN'T RUIN.

ARE YOU
DRUNK?

☐ YES

☐ NO

X

I'M looking FOR A BETTER LIFE. SUGGESTIONS?

DO YOU LOVE
ME ?

a . YES

b . a

c . b

GIVE ME
COFFEE
TO CHANGE THE
THINGS I
CAN AND WINE
TO ACCEPT
THOSE I
CANNOT.

WHAT ARE you
WAITING FOR?

MAKE it NOW!

STRESS
DOESN'T
REALLY
GO WITH
MY
OUTFIT.

I MISS

~~YOU~~

ME

IF YOU LOVE

SOMEONE

SET THEM FREE

IF THEY

DON'T COME BACK,

CALL THEM UP

LATER WHEN

YOU'RE

DRUNK

YOU
DEFINE
BEAUTY
YOURSELF

I'M NOT

ENTiRELy

HERE

THANK YOU

FOR BEING

MY UNPAID

THERAPIST

MY SEX LIFE
IS LIKE
COCA - COLA.

FIRST IT WAS NORMAL
THEN LIGHT AND
NOW IT'S
ZERO.

YOU

~~will~~ will

NEVER FIND

ANOTHER

ME.

IT'S OK
TO UNFOLLOW
PEOPLE IN
REAL LIFE.

WE ARE

ONLY

~~A MOMENT~~

A MOMENT

THIS SOCIETY

MAKES US

GOOGLE

ATTENTION!!!!

(THANKS FOR YOUR ATTENTION)

ONE MINUTE

DON'T READ

DON'T TALK

NO PHOTOS

JUST LOOK

... AND SEE

ME:

I HAVE

A

DREAM TO

FINISH

LOOK AROUND YOU.

APPRECIATE WHAT

YOU HAVE.

NOTHING WILL

BE THE SAME

IN A YEAR.

I NEED

A

HUG e AMOUNT

OF MONEY .

1) THINK

2) IDEA

3) TRY

4) DO

5) DO AGAIN

6) AND AGAIN

7) KEEP DOING

8) SUCCESS !

MOOD : FUCK

MY ANXIETIES
HAVE
ANXIETIES.

MAKE ART

NOT

CONTENT

WHY FALL IN LOVE,
WHEN YOU CAN
FALL ASLEEP.

KEEP TALKING

I'M DIAGNOSING

YOU.

CLOSED FOR

PRIVATE EVENT.

OUR APOLOGIES

TO DAY
BREAK

I EXPECT
NOTHING
AND I'M
still
DISAPPOINTED

WHO CARES
WHAT OTHER
PEOPLE THINK?

people no longer

READ ...

THEY WRITE.

4 HRS WITH
THE RIGHT PERSON
FEELS LIKE

3 MINUTES

SHALOM

SALAM

SALUT

PEACE

IT'S NOT
NECESSARY
TO REACT
TO
EVERYTHING
YOU NOTICE.

MAKE SURE
YOU'RE HAPPY
WITH YOUR LIFE
OFFLINE too.

WE'RE
GOING TO
NEED
A LOT OF
LOVE.

3 WISHES :

1) TO EARN MONEY
WITHOUT WORKING

2) TO LOVE WITHOUT
BEING HURT.

3) TO EAT WITHOUT
GETTING FAT.

ZZZZZZ ...

OK, I RESPECT

YOUR WRONG

OPINION.

TO DO LIST :

1) OVERTHINK

2) MISS SOMEONE
   I NEVER HAD

3) GO HAVE A
   SNACK

4) OVERTHINK

DO YOU   LOVE ME?

☐   OR   ☐

YES   YES

GO

SOMEPLACE

WHERE

NO ONE

KNOWS

YOUR

NAME.

LISTEN TO THE
BIRDS NOT
THE NEWS

2021 CHANGED ME

2022 BROKE ME

2023 OPENED MY EYES

2024 I'M COMING
        BACK!

— I love
TALKING
To you

EVEN IF
I HAVE
NOTHING to SAY.

BE A GOOD PERSON IN REAL LIFE, NOT ON SOCIAL MEDIA

INTELLIGENCE
IS SEXY

ME :

SOMETIMES

I TALK TO

MYSELF

ME ! OMG
SAME

FUCK YOU

I DID

MY BEST.

I'M TAKING A
BREAK FROM
MY MENTAL HEAlTH
TO FOCUS ON
MY SOCiAL MEDiA

NO INSPIRATION
TODAY,
SORRY

TODAY I WILL
LIVE IN THE
MOMENT

UNLESS THE MOMENT
IS UNPLEASANT
IN WHICH CASE I
WILL EAT A
CARROT CAKE.

NO SPACE

FOR NEW

MESSAGES

— SAY SOMETHING
    IN ITALIAN.

—   pizza?

THINGS I like:

- YOUR SMile

- YOUR VOICE

- YOUR EYES

- YOUR LAUGH.

- YOUR lips

KISS ME

BEFORE MY

BOYFRIEND

COMES BACK.

SAY "I LOVE YOU"

WITHOUT USING

THOSE THREE WORDS.

GO!

SORRY I'M LATE,

I DIDN'T

WANT TO

COME

NOBODY is too
BUSY ...

IT'S JUST

A MATTER
OF
PRIORITIES.

ARE WE
SUPPOSED
TO BE
JOYFULL ?

I'M GOOD
IN BED.

I CAN SLEEP

All DAY.

MAY WE
ALWAYS HAVE
THE MONEY TO
BUY THE
THINGS WE
SCREENSHOT.

I HAVE A CRUSH

AND IT'S NOT

YOU.

AM I PERFECT?
NO

BUT AM I
TRYING TO
BE A BETTER
PERSON ?

ALSO NO

– SO WE CAN
  TALK?

  – TALK ABOUT WHAT?

– US

  – WHY DO YOU
    WANNA TALK
    ABOUT THE
        UNITED STATES?

GOOD THINGS

HAPPEN WHEN

YOU SMILE

OR WHEN

YOU'RE

NAKED

WE WANT

PEACE !
.

YOUR KISS
WAS SO
REAL IN
MY DREAM

WHO SAYS
THE NIGHTS

ARE FOR
SLEEPING?

_ I LOVE YOU

_ I KNOW

SOCIAL MEDIA
HAS TURNED
THE ART OF
LIVING INTO
AN ACT OF
PERFORMANCE

STOP MALE
EGOS FROM
RUINING
THE FUTURE!

ONLINE ISN'T REAL

IT'S

~~BLACK~~

JUST

FRIDAY

I TRUST YOU WITH

MY PHONE

PASSWORD

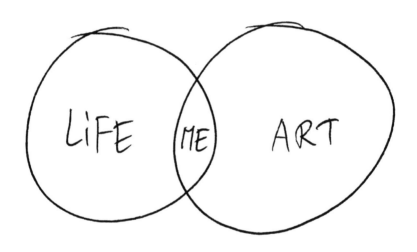

NOT EVERYONE
AT YOUR WORKPLACE
IS YOUR FRIEND

DO YOUR JOB
GET PAID
GO HOME.

I DON'T
KNOW
ANYTHING
BUT I
KNOW
I MISS YOU

– DAD, WHEN I
GROW UP, I
WANT TO BE
AN ARTIST.

– SON, YOU
CAN'T DO
BOTH.

— YOUR GENERATION
    IS ADDICTED
  TO ATTENTION.

  — I KNOW. IT'S LIKE
WE All WANT TO BE
  FAMOUS EVEN THOUGH
WE ARE NOT GOOD
AT ANYTHING.

:) ;

YOU

DECIDE

pLEASE

~~DON'T~~ DO NOT

DISTURB

I AM

DISTURBED

ENOUGH

ALREADY.

ME, AFTER

I SEND ONE

EMAIL:

WORLD PEACE

MULTIPLE ORGASMS

AND FANCY

BOXED CHOCOLATES.

IN THAT

ORDER.

I MIGHT LOOK INNOCENT BUT I SCREENSHOT A LOT!

IF YOU'RE

LOOKING

FOR A SIGN,

THIS IS IT.

JUST TO
WAIT UNTIL
THERE IS
NOTHING LEFT
TO WAIT FOR.

TAKING
CARE   OF
YOUR SELF
IS
PRODUCTIVE.

I'M SORRY

I ROASTED

YOU   I WAS

TRYING TO

FLIRT.

EVERYTHING
IS
AMAZING
AND

NoBoDY IS

HAppY.

THERE'S HOPE

BUT NOT

FOR US.

ADULT LIFE IS
CONSTANTLY SAYING
TO YOUR FRIENDS LET'S
DO SOMETHING ~~SOON~~
SOON

AND SUDDENLY
6 MONTHS HAVE
GONE BY.

YOU KNOW

WHAT'S SEXY?

A REAL

CONVERSATION

IF THIS IS

REALITY

I'M NOT

INTERESTED

READ A BOOK!

YOU'RE
ALIVE,

BUT ARE
YOU
LIVING?

It's
DIFFERENT,
I LiKE iT!

I DO
NOT OWE
YOU
AN
EXPLANATION

HOW

LONG

MUST I

WAIT

FOR

YOU ?

FIND
WHAT
YOU'D
DIE
FOR

WE THINK
TOO MUCH
AND FEEL
TOO
LITTLE.

Acknowledgements

Thank you to my family and to my followers, as well as to the entire Hodder publishing team.

About the Author

Thomas Lélu is a contemporary artist, photographer and author of fiction. His visual work has been exhibited in numerous galleries and museums around the world and he has published 5 novels including *Le Parisien* (Flammarion) but also essays such as *Le Manuel de la Photo Ratée* (Léo Scheer) and *After* (Sternberg Press). He trained at Ensad (National School of Decorative Arts), he first worked as a graphic designer for many years before pursuing his career in the fashion press and advertising. In 2020 he opened a first gallery in Paris, La Cité, which he directs and since 2022 he has been curator of the Hôtels Amour residences in Paris and Nice.

An artist with a nomadic practice, deliberately flirting with that of the amateur to better blur the lines and desecrate the status of the Contemporary Visual Artist, Thomas Lélu nevertheless adopts work protocols based on research, selection, extraction, the organization of images and words which constitute the material of his work, before diversion and transposition. This approach of quest, archiving and putting into perspective makes Thomas Lélu one of our archaeologists of the present time.

First published in Great Britain in 2024 by Hodder Catalyst
An imprint of Hodder & Stoughton
An Hachette UK company

1

A CIP catalogue record for this title is available from the British Library

Hardback ISBN 978 1 399 73612 1
eBook ISBN 978 1 39 973611 4

Publisher: Lauren Whelan
Senior Project Editor: Liv Nightingall
Designer: Hart Studio
Senior Production Controller: Matt Everett

Colour origination by Born Group
Printed and bound in China by C&C Offset Printing Co., Ltd.

Hodder & Stoughton policy is to use papers that are natural, renewable and
recyclable products and made from wood grown in sustainable forests. The logging
and manufacturing processes are expected to conform to the environmental
regulations of the country of origin.

Hodder Catalyst
Hodder & Stoughton Ltd
Carmelite House
50 Victoria Embankment
London
EC4Y 0DZ

www.hodder.co.uk